7 DAYS IN HELL: I WAS THERE!

An Eyewitness Account of the True Existence Hell

By Larry E."Buck" Hunter

7 Days In Hell: I Was There!
 An Eyewitness Account of the True Existence Hell

First Printing, 2014

Printed in the United States of America

PUBLISHED BY
ECONO PUBLISHING, LLC
6599 Kuna Road, Kuna, Idaho 83634
E-mail: econopublishing@gmail.com
Website: www.econopublishing.com

TABLE OF CONTENTS

7 DAYS IN HELL: I WAS THERE!

An Eyewitness Account of the True Existence Hell

By Larry E."Buck" Hunter

7 DAYS IN HELL BOOK TRAILER VIDEO
https://www.youtube.com/watch?v=iTaWjEdVfmU

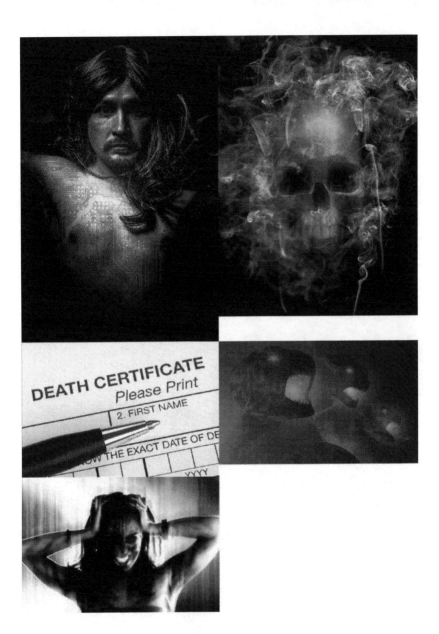

7 DAYS IN HELL: I WAS THERE!
An Eyewitness Account of the True Existence Hell

By Larry E."Buck" Hunter

I WAS THERE; HELL IS REAL. I had asked GOD to show me what Hell would be like. The dream – vision He gave me was so real, I actually thought I was there, in HELL, and not dreaming. I had to PRAY and shake it off. God said to me: "This dream vision was ONLY a glimpse of THE HORRORS HELL!" (Similar to Paul's vision of HEAVEN: 2 Corinthians 12:1-4)

The Dream-vision was a just a preview of what **ETERNITY WOULD BE LIKE WITHOUT GOD. HELL IS REAL!** (John 3:1-20)

There is that OCCASIONAL MOMENT when a person is in the RIGHT PLACE at the RIGHT TIME - these MOMENTS are RARE – but, when they OCCUR the RESULTS will LINGER for ETERNITY. Larry E. "Buck" Hunter

PREFACE

I was asked WHY? Why a book about Hell? Nobody goes to Hell by choice, however, most people do!

But, most people do not know there is a choice, one that is totally theirs. The best way I can really answer that question is to give you a brief history of my life.

I was sixty-six years old when I asked GOD to show me what it would be like to go to HELL!

MY FIRST EXPERINCE WITH DEATH

When I was around 13 my brother Jim and I worked on a farm with my stepfather. My stepfather was operating a big gas tractor.

There were two 50 gallon drums of gasoline In the back of my stepfather's pickup truck, used for servicing the tractor. My brother and I thought it would be fun to sniff the gas.

The next thing I know I am seeing my life played back to me like a film in reverse.   My whole life was coming back to me in waves like an accordion. Then, suddenly I was standing before the LORD JESUS and a great throne and He was surrounded by people. Then with a voice of utter authority, I heard the LORD speaking to the people who were there, "Depart from me, I never knew you. Your name is not in the book".

Before I could blink, massive Angels swooped down and threw those people into a burning lake of fire. At that instant I knew that lake was Hell. I felt my body begin to tremble and my knees were weak. As I stood there shaking, uncertain of my own fate, God looked directly into my eyes and spoke. "It is not your time to die. You must go back. I have work for you to do".

At that moment I heard EMT yelling; "Buck, Jim can you hear me?" Then someone saying "They are back!" As my mind swirled back into reality, I was hit with the realization that I, Buck Hunter had been there... before God in the Great Hall of Judgment.

THERE IS A CHOICE

Seven years later, when I was 20, I was in a terrifying car accident. It started out as any other normal Wednesday, but little did I know on that day my life was about to be changed forever. I needed a ride to pick up my car and a good friend was kind enough to oblige. With my girlfriend along, we hopped into the car he had just bought a 1966 Pontiac Hydro Convertible with 3 duce carburetors.

As we drove away he leaned over and said to me that he needed to stop by the restaurant/bar where his mom worked to pick up some money. When we stopped, my girlfriend and I waited in the car. At one point, I remember getting annoyed and I said something about him taking too long. Unbeknownst to us, while he was in the restaurant, he had downed 6 double shots.

I can't say I knew he was drinking but I did notice he seemed a little amped up. As he jumped into the car and shoved his key into the ignition, he announced, "Hang on. I am going to show you what this baby can do". The engine turned over with a mighty roar and growled eagerly as he revived it up to its full top end potential, and with that, we screeched out of the parking lot. I think the booze kicked at about the time we hit 125 mph and the front end of the car broke loose. We started weaving from side to side, just then he lost control, crossed the yellow line and smashed into a car parked on the other side of the street.

Like a domino effect we bounced off of one car and into another and Sailed out of control. The destruction seemed like it was never going to end. My ears were ringing with the sounds of twisting metal. By the time the car came to a stop, 7 other cars were totaled, one of them was a huge 1950 Hudson, which had been severed in two.

As I slowly came back into reality, I felt dizzy and confused. I tried to shake off the disorientation and get a handle on what had just happened; but the inside of the car was black and my eyes couldn't adjust to the darkness. I could feel warm blood oozing from my head and I felt a giant gash in my forehead. I knew I was in trouble because 4 of my fingers fit into the deep gaping hole in my head. I called out to my friends but there was no answer.

The car's engine was still racing and I smelled gasoline. I knew the car was going to explode. I had to get out fast. I felt around the twisted steel for an escape route. I decided my door was my best bet. The door was folded up like an accordion and I could not open it. So I laid on my back and kicked that door right off its hinges.

Once I got out of car, I tried to find my friends. I looked around and called for them both but once again, there was no answer. I didn't know it at the time but my girlfriend had been thrown through the windshield and was badly injured.

I feared that my friends were trapped inside the wreckage I went around to the trunk of the car, thinking maybe I could stop the gas leak. Just then my head burst open and blood began spurting out of my wound. I heard a loud voice booming in my ear, and it said these words "I will kill you this time. Jesus will not save you now".

I was filled with panic. Out of instinct, I began to run and I started yelling back to the voice, "You will not kill me, you will not kill me. God please save me"! No sooner had the words left my lips, the light poles started to act like projectiles. They were being pulled right up out of the ground and hurled at me like spears!

Dodging them, I just kept running and running. When I finally got my bearing; I saw I was at my

Aunt Billie and Uncle Charlie's house. I pounded on the door and tried with all of my might to get them to answer. I was desperate to call for help. Since both my aunt and uncle were nearly deaf, they did not hear the door. I collapsed and passed out in front of their door on the front porch. I woke up to the sound of sirens and I could see the flashing red lights.

They were close enough for me to hear one of the paramedics say: "There is a girl over here. I think she may be dead". Before I could respond I passed out again.

When I awoke it was around 4 am. I was still on my aunt and uncles porch. I decided that I better head to the hospital. When I got there, I learned that the police were waiting for me. Having found my blood spatters all over the trunk of the car, they had launched an all-out search for a badly injured, missing person.
I learned my girlfriend was in surgery with a nearly fatal head injury. They said she would live but was going to lose the sight in one eye. My friend, who had been driving the car had walked away without a scratch; but, he had told the police that I was the driver.

After a few rounds of questioning by the police, I was cleared because the window post on the passenger side of the car had just about taken my head off in the crash and it was smeared and splattered with my blood. Since my friend didn't even have a cut on his body, the blood had to be mine. So the police cleared me of any wrongdoing and I was free to go.

After the doctors sewed me up I was released from the hospital with instructions to follow up with my personal doctor in the morning. When I went to my doctor's office the next day I was immediately ordered back to the hospital. I protested loudly and told the doctor there was no way I could back to the hospital because I had plans. The premiere of "Follow That Dream", starring Elvis, was opening, and I had a date that night to see it, plus, my band had a gig to play the music a local dance. His reaction was swift and poignant: He picked up the phone, called the funeral home and told them "To make arrangements to pick up my body". I got the message loud and clear and agreed that very minute to go to the hospital.

Once I got all checked in the hospital I began to feel an enormous pressure building up in my head. It was like nothing I had ever felt before. I didn't know it yet but a blood vessel had ruptured in my brain. When the doctor came in and saw me, his face was ashen and in a sober voice he relayed the news that I was indeed dying; and there wasn't anything they could do but keep me comfortable.

My dad Jack, and his sister, my favorite Aunt Ida, were there in the room for the awful news. I remember feeling guilty that I was putting them through this horrible ordeal. Being a very devout Catholic, Aunt Ida's first response was to call the priest to give me the last rites. I vaguely remember the Priest entering the room and I was gone. Instantly, I found myself in Heaven again.

Heaven was a peaceful place and I really wanted to stay. I remember feeling comfort and joy. The kind of feeling you want to last forever. But my time in Heaven was limited because again, the Lord told me: "I have more work for me to do". And with that, I was sent back to my body; and after 17 days I woke up back in the world.

In my experiences, I have seen the Judgment and witnessed people thrown into Hell. Twice I have enjoyed the comforts of Heaven. During my life as a Christian, now going on 45 years, I have been asked many times; what is Heaven like? What is HELL like?

Since I know what Heaven is like I asked God what is Hell like? And that's where my witness to you begins.

FAST FORWARD TO THE YEAR 2010

Through an extreme set of events in my life, I found myself serving a 72 month sentence in a Federal Prison Camp for money laundering. I will go into that story another time.

While I was at prison camp, I ministered in the Camp Church. I had heard the phrase: WHY DON'T YOU JUST GO TO HELL. I made a point to the person that they shouldn't wish that fate on anybody. His response back was: "Well, why don't you tell us what Hell is like"?

So, in response, I wrote a message titled: SO YOU WANT TO GO TO HELL. I used all the Bible references I could find; and many men came to know the LORD because of that message.

There is a REAL HELL. I wanted to experience HELL in such a way that I would know how to explain it to another person. I wanted to explain it with such authority that people would want to know Jesus and not ever want to go there or have anyone they know and love to go there either. I prayed and asked the Lord to show me what being in Hell is really like.

When I asked for this Hell experience I had no thoughts of writing a book. The Holy Spirit has directed me to write down all I saw, heard and felt, and to let the WORLD KNOW – HELL IS REAL, I WAS THERE!

Larry E. "Buck" Hunter - 7 Days in HELL

Hebrews 9:27: And just as it is appointed for [all] men once to die, and after that the [certain] judgment.

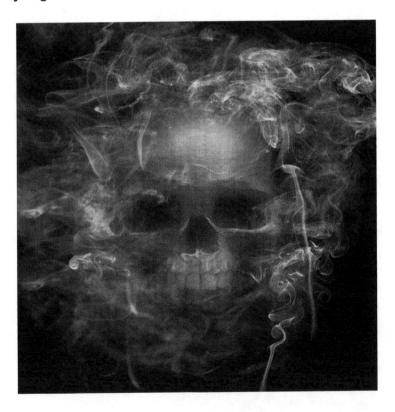

CHAPTER 1 THE DREAM

Matthew 7:13-14
Enter through the narrow gate. For wide is the gate and broad is the road that leads to destruction, and many enter through it. But small is the gate and narrow the road that leads to life, and only a few find it.

INTRODUCTION TO THE GIFT OF GODS SALVATION

Heaven operates by FAITH.

Hell operates by FEAR.

Ask yourself, "What is your greatest fear?"
For some of us it's spiders, rats, or snakes. For others, it's the thought of being burned to death, buried alive, murdered, tortured, or raped.

Focus for a moment on your deepest fear. Can you feel your neck hairs stand on end or your body shudder and your stomach turn? This FEAR is the fuel that ignites the fiery pits of Hell. Without Gods Salvation whatever your deepest fear is, is where your journey to Hell begins.

"As you read this discourse you will begin to understand what it will be like if you reject the free gift of salvation from God our Father". (1John 4:18).

I asked the LORD during a fast and prayer time to allow me to have a glimpse of HELL. I wanted to know exactly what would await a person who has rejected Christ and His GIFT of salvation.

I told the LORD that I wanted to be able to communicate to any living human being what awaits for them if they reject Jesus. I also asked for a better glimpse of Heaven, which I will tell you about later in the book.

So the LORD revealed to me in a dream like vision what the first 7 days in Hell would be like.

However, let me explain, in eternity there are no days, no time reference as we know them.

He told me in the vision that I would awake from my dream vision after experiencing 7 - 24 hour time periods of time in Hell.

This time frame would give me a reference in which anyone could understand just how terrifying Hell can be.

HEAVEN IS A REAL PLACE. HELL IS ALSO A REAL PLACE.

If you know the **LORD JESUS CHRIST** as Savior you WILL go to Heaven. If you do not know Him you WILL go to Hell.

The fact that Heaven is real and Hell is real was made very clear in the parable of Lazarus and the Rich Man. Both places were real.

You will be <u>conscious</u> in both Heaven and Hell. (Luke 16:19-31). One thing I want to make very clear is that GOD does not send anyone to Hell.

Heaven and Hell is our choice. God gave us Jesus and His FREE GIFT of GRACE and FREE will.

All we have to do is receive the Gift. In the Bible God said; **"This day I have set before you both LIFE and DEATH, therefore YOU CHOSE LIFE that you and your children may live.**
(Ephesians 2:5-10; Deuteronomy 30:11-20)

It is my sincerest desire that as you read this brief account of the horrors I experienced in Hell you will want the free gift of the Grace of God, and I will tell you how to get it.

Damnation or Salvation OUR CHOICE?

Heaven is a real place, and it exists in a real time.

Hell is also real place, which exists in a real time.

Mankind cherishes its conscious right to choose as one of the most valuable of our human rights, FREE will.

We choose what college to attend and what classes we'll take. Where to live, what we'll drive, the music we listen to and where to eat lunch. We choose whether to get out of bed early or stay up late at night. What clothes to wear or how to wear our hair.

LIFE IS ALL ABOUT THE CHOICES WE MAKE

Some say the very essence of living is in the moment to moment choices that we make for ourselves. We go about our days making thousands of choices. Some choices seem insignificant, while other choices change everything; but that's life isn't it?

The life we live in this world is crafted by each and every choice we make. It's so important to us to choose the path of our earthly life that so often we have neglected to consider the reality of death and the fact of eternal life.

Sooner or later, we all face the reality that one day, we too, shall die. We contemplate our deaths and make our choices.

Do we choose a burial plot or cremation? Should we buy insurance or write a will? We convince ourselves that our own death is inevitable and that it's not really important what we think about it because we'll be dead.

However, this is a TRUE FACT:
If you know the LORD JESUS CHRIST as Savior you WILL go to Heaven.

If you do not know Him you WILL go to Hell.

Both places were real. You will be conscious in both Heaven and Hell. (Luke 16:19-31)

CHAPTER 2

DAY 1: THE JOURNEY BEGINS

When a person dies his time in eternity begins. If you do not know the LORD, you will start your experience with a sinister presence as your spirit leaves your body and FEAR will begin to well up inside of you.

Your unsaved Spirit will depart from your body at the moment of your death, but, instead of being met by an Angel, you will be met with evil. A demon will take hold of you with HIS claw-like hands. (Psalm 116:3)

Suddenly the HORROR of what is happening fills your Spirit. The scent of death now fills your nostrils with its stench. You try to fight back but no matter how you much you scream for help, no one will come.

THERE IS NO HELP FOR THE DAMNED.

Upon your death, you can still see your dead body and the other people that may be there; but they cannot hear your cries for help.
(Luke 16:23-25; Acts 2:27; Revelation 6:8; Revelation 20:13-15)

YOU ARE NOW THE PROPERTY OF HELL. (Psalm 9:15-17)

Often a person will get prior notice of their trip into the afterlife. A doctor may tell them the horrible news that they only have a few days or months to live.

But, for most of us, the trip will begin without any notice at all-Heart attack, car accident, gun shot. However your death happens, your trip into the afterlife will begin at that very moment.

1.78 persons make this trip into eternity every second. Average 107 deaths per minute. 365 days per year. That means over 56,000,000 people will make this journey each year.

For many people, death arrives instantly. NO WARNING! One second you are alive and breathing, and the next moment your journey to either Heaven or Hell begins. (Psalm 55:15)

The Bible says: "That it is appointed for everyone to die and after that is the judgment". If you know Jesus as Savior, the Bible says; "To be absent from the body is to be present with the LORD". The flip side of that statement is, if you do not know the LORD JESUS, you will be present with the Devil and his angels in HELL. (Psalm 9:15-17; 2 Corinthians 5:8-9; Psalm 16:10).

When you begin your journey there is no need to make return plans. You are going to a place called Eternity. It is a one way trip. There are no returns. No DO OVER'S. No making it right. There is no coming back!

Your new life is now spiritual and it exists in a place called Eternity. Your new life has begun as you pass through the door marked Death. (Proverbs 15:10-11).

As I was shown Hell, my initial reaction was more than just frightening: Complete and utter darkness. My first thought was "What am I doing here? I was a good person! This can't be true".

But with each passing eternal moment the darkness becomes more intense. Fear starts to well up. **MY FEARS.**

I tried to renew my positive mental attitude. This is not happening to me. Where is my Faith? But there is no Faith. I was always positive. Try as I may ONLY FEAR came forth. My mind started to burn with red hot fear. Like seeing my life in reverse, every fear I ever had or thought of was now hitting me with the burning speed of light.

I tried to muster up a positive thought; but NOTHING, only FEAR filled my entire being. The darkness became blackness and more intense. There was No joy, No laughter, No music. NOTHING BUT FEAR. (Proverbs 1:26-27)

Then, as I started to move through the darkness, fear again blocked out everything. No positive thoughts. Oh, how it started to hurt. A mental pain greater than anything I had ever experienced. IT HURTS. Pain so intense and so bad. I screamed for help. No sounds came out. My screams were swallowed up by the utter darkness and total fear. I struggled to move, but I could not tell if I was moving forward, backwards, sideways or up and down. I had no reference points, only the sensation that I was falling. I was stripped of everything and felt nothing but the total and absolute darkness and fear.

(Matthew 8:12, Jude 1:6)

I began to hear faint and distant sounds. I thought maybe there is hope. Please somebody help me. I called out, HELP ME, HELP ME, please anybody. The only responses were the sounds of moans, groans and shrieks of terror.

I just continued to fall, and be filled with even more pain and agony. Fear was coming at me from every direction. All I could hear was the sounds of total fear coming at me through the darkness.

Suddenly, I bumped into something. What is it I thought? Another spirit maybe? I was wrong. It was total fear and absolute agony coming to greet me. And the moans, groans and shrieks of pain began coming from everywhere and every direction all at once.

I could feel the heat is like a blast furnace. NO LIGHT, only scalding hot black darkness. I felt like I am suffocating. Clouds of black dense smoke filled my lungs. The heat and blackness were intolerable. (Psalm 11:6) What day is this? I tried to think.

IT FELT LIKE FOREVER, BUT THIS IS ONLY THE FIRST DAY OF FOREVER!!

CHAPTER 3

DAY 2: THE JOURNEY CONTINUES

I could feel Fear, only Fear. Let's say that one of your biggest fears in life was being buried alive. All of a sudden you are now clawing at the lid of the coffin. Your mind is bursting with the pain of sheer panic. Red hot searing pain pierces your brain.

This is what it was like for me. Only fear remained in my mind. I could feel nothing else. I tried scream for help but no help would ever come. There is no escaping Hell.

I was crying for help. Scratching the coffin lid. No one hears me. I cannot get out. HELP, HELP Please God, I begged. **Only there is No help from GOD. He is not there.** No answers, only panic and fear.

I kept screaming for help. Pleading for help. No HELP, only FEAR rules here.

I started to feel little worms, spiders and bugs. They were slightly glowing like a lighting bug. Glowing like the light given off from the soft sulfur glow in underground caverns, and it smelled strong like a sulfur match. Some of the bugs morphed into little demons. Some of the bugs and spiders had twisted human faces. They laughed as they began to sting me and burrow into my spiritual flesh.

There is no way to even describe how horrible this experience was.

These soft glowing demon bugs dancing, laughing and taunting me with their words: **"Where is Your God now?** He is nowhere to be found. You are ours for all eternity". My ears were filled with no other sounds but their ugly laughter. **(Revelation 20:10)**. (**Psalms 10:5**)

I tried to gain perception inside of the total darkness but all I could feel was the sensation that the coffin was closing in on me. Shrinking smaller and smaller, I thought, will I run out of air? My mind was on fire. The heat of this place is absolutely unbearable. I crave a drink of water. Just a drop to cool my tongue. Then I remembered the story of the rich man and Lazarus - why did I not listen?
Just a drop of water, please somebody please. I begged out loud. The air just seems to be getting thicker. I know it now. I am suffocating.

I scratched, screamed, begged and pleaded. NO HELP. My mind was searing with white hot FEAR. I screamed and clawed some more. But all that reflected back to me was my fear and terror.

I heard a sound. I thought maybe help was finally here. It wasn't any help at all, instead it was what sounded like millions of spirit people screaming out for help. I could sense each of them was dealing with their own individual fears. They too needed help, but no help comes in Hell.

ONLY FEAR. My thoughts turned back to myself: What day is this?

But it was only Day 2 of forever.
(Revelation 14:11)

CHAPTER 4

DAY 3: TOTAL DEPRIVATION

Day 3 begins now, but days are only an illusion in this place because really there is no time frame in eternity. Counting the days was a luxury that God allowed my mind to keep track of my time in Hell.

I just kept saying to myself, this is not happening, it's only a bad dream. I will wake up soon.

Then, I can feel someone lurking nearby me. **"LEAVE ME ALONE"**.

I thought for a moment maybe it was GOD. "Oh God please help me. Please get me out of here". But then I heard only the ugly, mocking laugh of those bug-like demons: **"Your GOD is not here. He cannot help you. We own you. We are your gods now"**. Fear heaped upon more fear is all I could feel.

The sounds of weeping and the gnashing of what sounded like teeth filled my senses. It got louder and louder and I realized that there was millions of people there. I could not see anyone in the utter darkness and all I hear is the terror of their fears.

The sounds of their fear are deafening. There is no one will help them. Nobody to help me. Nobody can help anybody.

Every spirit here going through their own private, fearful, spiritual Hell. Totally controlled and fueled by their OWN FEAR here in the utter darkness where the heat is intolerable.

The utter darkness along with every fear I have ever known or could ever imagine now controlling my spirit mind.

TOTAL FEAR! People having their spiritual bodies ripped apart by demons. The demons laugh with mocking glee. I can do nothing, just listen in horror to what is happening.

I feel nothing else except starvation and thirst. There's no way to satisfy or quench it: Total deprivation, wanting and suffering. In my mind I think, what day is this? I've got to know, what day is this? **OH GOD. GOD, I screamed but GOD not here, and no one to hear my cries.**

IT IS ONLY DAY 3 OF ETERNITY.
(Revelation 11-18, 20:10)

CHAPTER 5

DAY 4: HELL IS NO PARTY

I remember when I used to joke, if I went to Hell I certainly wouldn't be lonely. Just about everyone has made a remark like that.

"All my friends will be there and we will party like there is no tomorrow". Everybody would be laughing, having fun, let's have another drink.

YOU'RE RIGHT ABOUT ONE THING, THERE IS NO TOMORROW.

HELL is not a party. As far as a drink, I would give anything just to have one drop of water to cool my mouth. (Luke 16:24, 28)

I think that maybe I can recognize some of the spirit voices I hear. I try to talk but nobody seems to hear me. All I hear is the sound of uncontrollable weeping, screaming for help and the gnashing of teeth.

No help for anyone. (Matthew 25:30) Only absolute despair.

When is this nightmare going to stop?

When will I wake up? I think to myself: Am I dreaming?

Then I realize I am awake, there is no sleep, no rest.

THIS IS FOREVER!
And It Is Only Day 4.
(Revelation 14:11)

CHAPTER 6

DAY 5: FEAR ONLY FEAR

As day 5 begins, I think if I could only get a message home! Warn my family and friends about this place. If I could only tell them how wrong I was. . . . .

How sorry I am for making fun of Christian people. Nobody should have to come here. (Luke 16:26-31)

Then my thoughts return back to FEAR. That is all there is here, FEAR and more FEAR.

No LOVE, only HATE.

No relief, it seems to being getting darker and darker. The heat is getting hotter and hotter. (Isaiah 33:14)

Then my fear for my loved ones comes crashing back on me. Just the thought of a loved one, or even a friend, or anyone coming here is so painful.

The pain of that thought is unbearable. Every rational thought is always with fear.

NO RELIEF.

Even what could be a positive thought immediately turns to fear.

Total futileness - FEAR only FEAR.

Now I hear more screaming for help. More gnashing of teeth.

NO HELP. More and more darkness. More and more heat. My mind says, what time is it? What day is this? **Then fear returns! It is only day 5.** (Matthew 13:36-43)

CHAPTER 7

DAY 6: GOODNESS DOES NOT EXIST IN HELL

DAY 6 BEGINS. There is no goodness in this place, only terror, misery, horror and fear. There is no peace, no sleep, no food and no water. There is no help in this unholy place.

No light shines through anywhere, there is only darkness. I think to myself, if I could only die. I long for death, I pray for death, a way out.

Then it comes back to me again. I am dead, this is real, I missed it, and I am in Hell, forever! (Matthew 18:7-9).

Suddenly every evil or fearful thought I have ever had comes screaming back at me. Amplified a million times over, reverberating through my mind and completely consuming soul. Only evil exists now in my spirit. There is a total absence of love or care, a total absence of light.

NO HEAVENLY FATHER. NO GOODNESS EXISTS HERE IN HELL. (Matthew 25:41-46)

Cries for help are coming from everywhere. Cries that will go unanswered forever. No help.

No relief. Only more intense heat fueled by my own evil nature, and that nature is fueled by fear. Evil so strong that I could have never imagined it when I was alive on earth.

I think to myself once again, why didn't I listen? Why did I reject the FREE GIFT OF SALVATION? Why did I reject Jesus? (Acts 4:12; Matthew 25:30)

Just the very thought of the name Jesus shoots extreme pain through my spirit. Oh, why didn't I listen?

RIGHT THEN I was overcome by the booming and terrifying voice of Satan as he screams, *"That NAME cannot be spoken of here, I am your god now. You will worship me only".* Will this ever end?   What day is this? *Seems like it has been forever. It is!* IT'S ONLY DAY 6.

CHAPTER 8

DAY 7: HELL IS FOREVER

Today I seem to be sensing the presence of a new spirit person. "Why am I here", his spirit seemed to ask? "What is this place? Why am I here" he asked again? "I thought I was saved. I went to church all my life. Why am I here"?

The terror in his spirit was immense. Fear was starting to rip into his spirit mind. I tried to speak but nothing would come out. Only his sense of terror, evil and fear were all I could feel. I couldn't help him. I felt so helpless. (Romans 3:10-18)

In the deep darkness I could see the soft glow of scorpion like creatures with distorted human faces. Dimly illuminated, they were laughing and sneering. They stung and bit our spirits with their piercing stingers and sharp fangs. The pain of the stings are so dreadful I cannot find the words to explain the agony I felt.

Millions and millions of these creatures began swooping down upon us all. Swarms were biting and stinging everyone.

The screams of terror and pain were such a horrific and deafening sounds. The screams of the multitude sounds like rolling thunder. But the bugs didn't care about our screams, they just kept right on biting and stinging, tormenting, laughing and sneering.

As quickly as the scorpion creatures appeared the swarms went away, but every few hours they would return. Each time they returned their stings and bites were even more severe.

I thought in my spirit, what is wrong with me? I was always helpful and good to everyone. Then I realized there is no good in me. Only the evil, the evil nature of the father of lies, Satan himself, is my nature now. Only his unholy spirit is existing inside of me.

Fear, terror, and every ugliness that could exist is taking over my spirit.
(Ephesians 2:1-3; John 8:43-44)

I was so hopeful I could help this new spirit, but I cannot find hope, hope does not exist in my spirit anymore. It hurts, oh how this hurts. There is no hope in me. Only fear. Only Evil.

This is the truth. This is forever. There will never be an end to this and this thought only amplifies my fears.

Each day this terror gets stronger and stronger and it strangles out any of the good that was once part of me. There is nothing left for me now. Only more darkness, more heat. More screams of terror and agony. (**Revelation 14:10–11**)

I think again, but only for a fleeting instant. Why did I not listen? So many times I had been warned. So many times I had heard the message of the free gift of salvation. I had rejected it. Even laughed at it over and over again. I was a fool.

My memories came reeling back in a flood of my rejections of Salvation, mocking me. I had so many chances. Of every decision I'd ever made, I rejected the most important one of all.

Someone would ask if I had been saved. I would brush it off. ***"Saved from what, save yourself"! I would always exclaim,*** making fun of them for their ignorance. I was smug and thought I was so smart.

Time after time, Father God had sent someone to tell me about His free gift of salvation. Each time I

had rationalized and rejected the message and the messenger.
((John 12:41-48; Luke 16:27-31))

Now I cannot even hold a thought of goodness. I try to remember the saving grace of the words they had spoken to me but nothing, only empty despair.

What could have been goodness and salvation has now turned to terror and fear.

Oh, why didn't I listen? What time is it? Will I ever wake up from this nightmare? Then, once again the demons of fear laugh and scowl in my face.

I realize, THIS IS FOREVER!
ITS ONLY DAY 7.

CHAPTER 9

THE NIGHTMARE ENDS

I AM AWAKE, my eyes are open. I blink and blink again. I touch my body. Am I still alive? Am I still here, on earth, still alive! There is still a chance.

I had asked GOD to show me what Hell would be like. The dream-vision was so real! I know I was there, in HELL, and that it had not been a dream.

I had to PRAY with all of my strength just to try to shake it off.

<u>God said to me that this dream vision was a gift and merely a glimpse of WHAT "DOES NOT" have to happen.</u>

CHAPTER 10

WHAT HAPPENS WHEN WE DIE?

When we die our spirit leaves our body. We will become instantly aware of the spirit realm. It will be as real to us as the earthly realm is now. We will have all 5 of our senses working, actually working better than they did when were in the flesh. (See Lazarus and the Rich Man) Our 5 senses, sight, touch, smell, hearing and taste will remain. (Luke 16:19-31; 2 Corinthians 5:6-8)

If we are reborn before we die, our reborn spirit will be functioning near the speed of light. Totally free from the encumbrances of our flesh body. We will suddenly find ourselves in Heaven.

As a born again person - SPIRIT, to be absent from the body is to be present with the LORD in Heaven. (2 Corinthians 5:6-8 Amplified)
So then, we are always full of good and hopeful and confident courage; we know that while we are at home in the body, we are abroad from the home with the Lord [that is promised us]. For we walk by faith [we [a]regulate our lives and conduct ourselves by our conviction or belief respecting man's relationship to God and divine things, with trust and holy fervor; thus we walk] not by sight or appearance. [Yes] we have confident and hopeful courage and are pleased rather to be away from home out of the body and be at home with the Lord.

Our spirit will not be a shapeless vapor as the world sometimes portrays. We will have the same form as our material body. Our flesh body was only an outer covering for our spirit, much like a glove covering a hand.

When we die and leave our flesh body behind we will look much like we did when were alive in our flesh body. Our body will be glorious. Everything in the Heavenly realm is far superior to the natural earthly realm.
(John 20:19-20; John 20:24-29; Luke 24:36-43)

WE TEND TO DOUBT THAT THE INVISIBLE SPIRIT REALM EXISTS. *IT DOES, WHETHER YOU BELIEVE NOW OR NOT.*

We, for the most part, tend to deny any reality we cannot experience with our 5 senses.

We may not be able to see the Heavenly realm with our natural eyes; however, as a born again person, we can see it through the eye of Faith. Seeing things through the eye of Faith that cannot be seen in the natural realm is another gift from God.

The spiritual realm is eternal, forever. In it you are **BORN AGAIN** through the free gift of grace with which you will **live in heaven**. If you are not **BORN AGAIN**, then you **WILL LIVE IN HELL FOREVER.** (Revelation 21:6-8; Revelation 20:10-15)

As born again Christians we are looking forward to the day when we will exchange our flesh body for the permanent glorified one that we will have when we go to Heaven to live with our Father and Jesus forever.

Our body will be both spiritual and natural. We will be able to operate in both the natural and the spiritual realms.

When Jesus rose from the dead and ascended to Heaven and then returned for 40 days, He returned in HIS glorified body. Jesus could easily move from the spiritual realm and to the natural realm and then back to the spiritual realm.

He appeared to His disciples at what seemed right out of the air: Walking right through a locked door or a wall, and then vanishing again just as quickly. (John 20:19-20; John 20: 24-28)

He said to his disciples, touch me, handle me, behold my hands and feet, for a spirit does not have flesh and bones, as you can plainly see that I have. (Luke 24:37)

CHAPTER 11

HOW TO NOT GO TO HELL

I want to make it very clear right here and now. I am not trying to get you to go to church. Stop smoking. Stop drinking. Stop cussing, or anything else that has to do with your current life.

The Bible says, we all have sinned. Going to Heaven is not about these things. They may enter in later, but those things have nothing to with whether or not you go to Heaven.

It used to bug me so much when someone would approach me and begin to tell me about everything **I WOULD HAVE TO GIVE UP.** *I will endeavor to tell you only what's most important and that is how to go to Heaven.*

It will be up to you, through the Word of God and the Holy Spirit, how you will choose to live your life.

I am not trying to change your life. I am trying to save your soul!

Going to Heaven is a FREE GIFT, the ticket has already been purchase by someone else, JESUS, on your behalf. All you have to do is receive and use it.

THE BIBLE SAYS THAT JESUS ALREADY PAID THE PRICE FOR ALL SIN.

IT IS NOW A FREE GIFT TO ALL THOSE WHO WILL RECEIVE IT.

The Benefits of becoming a Christian are immense. They certainly out number all of the reasons to not become a Christian.
(Psalm 103:1-5)

A PRAYER TO RECEIVE

JESUS CHRIST AS SAVIOR

To receive your ticket to Heaven all you have to do is ask for it. If you are sincere about going to Heaven and not spending eternity in Hell, then PRAY this PRAYER:

Heavenly Father, I come to you in the Name of Jesus. Your word says, "Whosoever shall call on the name of LORD JESUS shall be saved" and "if you shall confess with your mouth the LORD JESUS, and believe in your heart that GOD raised HIM from the DEAD you will be saved." Father God - I take you at your word and thank you for the forgiveness of my sins and the FREE GIFT OF GRACE for SALVATION. I confess right now with my mouth that Jesus is LORD, and believe in my heart that JESUS is YOUR SON. I call on HIS NAME and CONFESS with my MOUTH that you have raised HIM from the dead. Father God, I am asking to be to be forgiven of my sins and to be saved.

Thank you Father for Jesus and the Holy Spirit coming into my heart and saving me. I ask this is Jesus Name - Amen. (Romans 10:8-13)

ROMANS 10:8-13

[8] But what does it say? The Word (God's message in Christ) is near you, on your lips and in your heart; that is, the Word (the message, the basis and object) of faith which we preach,

[9] *Because if you acknowledge and confess with your lips that Jesus is Lord and in your heart believe (adhere to, trust in, and rely on the truth) that God raised Him from the dead, you will be saved.*

[10] *For with the heart a person believes (adheres to, trusts in, and relies on Christ) and so is justified (declared righteous, acceptable to God), and with the mouth he confesses (declares openly and speaks out freely his faith) and confirms [his] salvation.*

[11] The Scripture says, No man who believes in Him [who adheres to, relies on, and trusts in Him] will [ever] be put to shame *or* be disappointed.

[12] [No one] for there is no distinction between Jew and Greek. The same Lord is Lord over all [of us] and He generously bestows His riches upon all who call upon Him [in faith].

[13] *FOR EVERYONE WHO CALLS UPON THE NAME OF THE LORD [INVOKING HIM AS LORD] WILL BE SAVED.*

CHAPTER 12 THE BENEFIT

If you have prayed this prayer the BIBLE says that you are saved. This means you will go to HEAVEN and not to HELL. We are spiritual beings, and our spirit will live for eternity. Jesus said, "I go away to prepare a place for you. If it were not true I would have told you. There are many mansions in my Father's house".
(John 14:1-4)

Heaven is a real place. It will be our home for eternity if we know Jesus as Savior. On the cross Jesus told one of the men who were being crucified, after this man asked Jesus to remember him when He came into His kingdom, "THIS DAY YOU WILL BE WITH ME IN PARADISE." (Luke 23:42-43). Jesus said "It is the Father's good pleasure to give us the Kingdom".

Heaven is a place of happiness. It will be even more real than our home here on earth.
(Revelation 21:10-27; Revelation 22:1-5; Luke 12:32).

There is that occasional moment when a person is in the right place at the right time - these moments are rare - but when they occur the results will linger for eternity.
Larry E. "Buck" Hunter

If you are born again, Heaven is where you will go. The home for all of us who have made Jesus their LORD and SAVIOR. Remember, it is appointed for all mankind to once die and after that, the judgment.

We are all moving along to that point, HEAVEN or HELL. The CHOICE is yours to make. Don't take another breath until you choose to make JESUS the LORD of YOUR LIFE.
(Deuteronomy 30:8-20).

IS HELL A REAL PLACE?

Our curiosity about the abode of the dead is not completely explained by biblical terms or verses. What we do know is that either eternal torment in Hell or eternal joy in Heaven awaits everyone after death, based on whether they trust in Christ's payment for sin or reject Christ.

The Bible calls Hell dark, lonely and miserable – a place of eternal separation from God. But God doesn't want anyone to go there. He wants a relationship with us through His Son, Jesus Christ, so we can spend eternity with Him in Heaven. You don't have to fear Hell. Take time now to be assured of your place in Heaven.

1. God Loves You And Has A Plan For You!

The Bible says, "God so loved the world that He gave His one and only Son, [Jesus Christ], that whoever believes in Him shall not perish, but have eternal life" (John 3:16-20). Jesus said, "I came that they may have life and have it abundantly". (John 10:10).

> "The thief comes to steal, kill, and destroy:
> I am come that they might have LIFE,
> and that they might have it more abundantly."
> - JESUS (John 10:10)

2. Man Is Sinful And Separated From God.

We have all done, thought or said bad things, which the Bible calls "sin." The Bible says, "All have sinned and fall short of the glory of God"

(Romans 3:21-26). "The result of sin is death, spiritual separation from God". (Romans 6:20-23).

3. God Sent His Son To Die For Our Sins!
Jesus died in our place so we could live with Him in eternity. "God demonstrates His own love toward us, in that while we were yet sinners, Christ died for us". (Romans 5:6-11). But it didn't end with His death on the cross. He rose again and still lives!

"Christ died for our sins. ... He was buried. ... He was raised on the third day, according to the Scriptures." (1 Corinthians 15:3-11). Jesus is the only way to God. Jesus said, **"I am the way, and the truth, and the life; no one comes to the Father, but through me". (John 14:5-7).**

TRUE FACTS

(1) Everyone will exist eternally either in Heaven or Hell (Daniel 12:2-3; Matthew 25:45-46; John 5:25-29; Revelation 20:14-15)

(2) Everyone has only one life in which to determine their destiny (Hebrews 9:23-28).

(3) Heaven or Hell is determined by whether a person believes (puts their trust) in Christ alone to save them (John 3:16-20, 36).

FACTS ABOUT HELL

(1) Hell was designed originally for Satan and his demons (Matthew 25:41-46; Revelation 20:10).

(2) Hell will also punish the sin of those who reject Christ (Matthew 13:41-43, 49-50; Revelation 20:11-15; 21:6-8)

(3) Hell is conscious torment.
Matthew 13:49-50 "furnace of fire...weeping and gnashing of teeth"

Mark 9:48 "where their worm does not die, and the fire is not quenched"
Revelation 14:9-101 "he will be tormented with fire and brimstone"

(4) Hell is eternal and irreversible.

Revelation 14:11 "the smoke of their torment goes up forever and ever and they have no rest day and night"

Revelation 20:14 "This is the second death, the lake of fire"

Revelation 20:15 "If anyone's name was not found written in the book of life, he was thrown into the lake of fire".

WRONG BELIEFS ABOUT HELL

(1) The second chance view – After death there is still a way to escape Hell.
Answer: "It is appointed unto men once to die and after that the judgment" (Hebrews 9:27).

(2) Universalism – All are eternally saved.
Answer: It denies the truth of salvation through Christ which means that a person decides to either trust in Christ or else he/she rejects Christ and goes to Hell (John 3:16-21;36).

(3) Annihilationist – Hell means a person dies like an animal – ceases to exist.
Answer: It denies the resurrection of the unsaved (John 5:25-28; etc. – see above). It denies conscious torment (see above).

OBJECTIONS ABOUT HELL

(1) A loving God would not send anyone to a horrible place like Hell.

Response: God is just (Romans 2:11).

God has provided the way of salvation to all (John 3:16, 17; 2 Corinthians 5:14, 15; 1 Timothy 2:6; 4:10; Titus 2:11; 2 Peter 3:9).

Even those who haven't heard of Christ are accountable for God's revelation in nature (Romans 1:20). God will seek those who seek Him (Matthew 7:7; Luke 19:10).

Therefore God doesn't send people to Hell, they choose it (Romans 1:18-32).

(2) Hell is too severe a punishment for man's sin. Response: God is holy-perfect (1 Peter 1:14-15). Sin is willful opposition to God our creator (Romans 1:18-32).

Our sin does merit Hell (Romans 1:32; 2:2).

What is unfair and amazing is that Christ died for our sins and freely offers salvation to all. (Romans 2:4; 3:21-26; 4:7, 5:6-11).

Biblical Terms Describing Where the Dead Are
Sheol - a Hebrew term simply describing "the grave" or "death" – Does not refer to "Hell" specifically.

Hades - A Greek term that usually refers to Hell – a place of torment. (Luke 10:15; 16:22-24).

Gehenna - A Greek term (borrowed from a literal burning dump near Jerusalem) that always refers to Hell – a place of torment.
(Matthew 5:30; 23:33).

"Lake of fire"- the final abode of unbelievers after they are resurrected. (Revelation 20:14, 15).

"Abraham's bosom" - (Luke 16:22) a place of eternal comfort.

"Paradise" - (Luke 23:43) a place of eternal comfort.

"With the Lord" - a key phrase describes where church age believers are after death. (Philippians 1:23; 1 Thessalonians 4:17; 2 Corinthians 5:8).

"New Heavens and earth" – where believers will be after they are resurrected.
(Revelation 20:4-6; 21:1-4).

MY NOTES & THOUGHTS

AUTHOR NOTES & THOUGHTS

I HAD TO PRAY AND SHAKE IT OFF. GOD SAID TO ME, THIS DREAM VISION WAS ONLY A GLIMPSE OF THE HORRORS HELL!

SIMILAR TO PAUL'S VISION OF HEAVEN: 2 CORINTHIANS 12:1-4

[1] TRUE, THERE is nothing to be gained by it, but [as I am obliged] to boast, I will go on to visions and revelations of the Lord.

[2] I know a man in Christ who fourteen years ago--whether in the body or out of the body I do not know, God knows--was caught up to the third Heaven.

[3] And I know that this man--whether in the body or away from the body I do not know, God knows-

[4] was caught up into paradise, and he heard utterances beyond the power of man to put into words, which man is not permitted to utter.

THE DREAM-VISION WAS A JUST A PREVIEW OF WHAT ETERNITY WOULD BE LIKE WITHOUT GOD.

HELL IS REAL!

YOU MUST BE BORN AGAIN
John 3:1-20

[1] There was a man of the Pharisees named Nicodemus, a ruler of the Jews.

[2] This man came to Jesus by night and said to Him, "Rabbi, we know that you are a teacher come from God; for no one can do these signs that you do unless God is with him."

[3] Jesus answered and said to him, "Most assuredly, I say to you, unless one is born again, he cannot see the kingdom of God."

[4] Nicodemus said to Him, "How can a man be born when he is old? Can he enter a second time into his mother's womb and be born?"

[5] Jesus answered, "Most assuredly, I say to you, unless one is born of water and the Spirit, he cannot enter the kingdom of God.

[6] "That which is born of the flesh is flesh, and that which is born of the Spirit is spirit.

[7] "Do not marvel that I said to you, 'You must be born again.

[8] "The wind blows where it wishes, and you hear the sound of it, but cannot tell where it comes from and where it goes. So is everyone who is born of the Spirit."

⁹ Nicodemus answered and said to Him, "How can these things be?"

¹⁰ Jesus answered and said to him, "Are you the teacher of Israel, and do not know these things?

¹¹ "Most assuredly, I say to you, we speak what we know and testify what we have seen, and ⱼ you do not receive our witness.

¹² "If I have told you earthly things and you do not believe, how will you believe if I tell you Heavenly things?

¹³ "No one has ascended to Heaven but He who came down from Heaven, that is, the Son of Man who is in Heaven.

¹⁴ "And as Moses lifted up the serpent in the wilderness, even so must the Son of Man be lifted up,

¹⁵ "that whoever believes in Him should not perish but have eternal life.

FOR GOD SO LOVED THE WORLD

¹⁶ "For God so loved the world that He gave His only begotten Son, that whoever believes in Him should not perish but have everlasting life.

¹⁷ "For God did not send His Son into the world to condemn the world, but that the world through Him might be saved.

¹⁸ "He who believes in Him is not condemned; but he who does not believe is condemned already, because he has not believed in the name of the only begotten Son of God.

[19] "And this is the condemnation, that the light has come into the world, and men loved darkness rather than light, because their deeds were evil. [20] "For everyone practicing evil hates the light and does not come to the light, lest his deeds should be exposed.

When I asked for this HELL experience I had no thoughts of writing a book. The HOLY SPIRIT has directed me to write down all I saw, heard and felt, and to let the WORLD KNOW – HELL IS REAL. Larry E. "Buck" Hunter - 7 Days in HELL

Hebrews 9:27: And just as it is appointed for [all] men once to die, and after that the [certain] judgment-

REDEMPTION THROUGH THE BLOOD OF CHRIST

[11] But Christ came as High Priest of the good things to come, with the greater and more perfect tabernacle not made with hands, that is, not of this creation.

[12] Not with the blood of goats and calves, but with His own blood He entered the Most Holy Place [t] once for all, having obtained eternal redemption.

[13] For if the blood of bulls and goats and the ashes of a heifer, sprinkling the unclean, sanctifies for the purifying of the flesh,

[14] how much more shall the blood of Christ, who through the eternal Spirit offered Himself without spot to God, cleanse your conscience from dead works to serve the living God?

[15] And for this reason He is the Mediator of the new covenant, by means of death, for the redemption of the transgressions under the first covenant, that those who are called may receive the promise of the eternal inheritance.

[16] For where there is a testament, there must also of necessity be the death of the testator.

[17] For a testament is in force after men are dead, since it has no power at all while the testator lives.

[18] Therefore not even the first covenant was dedicated without blood.

[19] For when Moses had spoken every precept to all the people according to the law, he took the blood of calves and goats, [f] with water, scarlet

wool, and hyssop, and sprinkled both the book itself and all the people,

20 saying, "This is the _h_ blood of the covenant which God has commanded you."

21 Then likewise he sprinkled with blood both the tabernacle and all the vessels of the ministry.

22 And according to the law almost all things are purified with blood, and _j_ without shedding of blood there is no remission.

23 Therefore it was necessary that _k_ the copies of the things in the Heavens should be purified with these, but the Heavenly things themselves with better sacrifices than these.

24 For Christ has not entered the holy places made with hands, which are _12_ copies of the true, but into Heaven itself, now to appear in the presence of God for us;

25 not that He should offer Himself often, as the high priest enters the Most Holy Place every year with blood of another –

26 He then would have had to suffer often since the foundation of the world; but now, once at the end of the ages, He has appeared to put away sin by the sacrifice of Himself.

27And as it is appointed for men to die once, but after this the judgment,

28 so _r_ Christ was offered once to bear the sins of many. To those who eagerly wait for Him He will appear a second time, apart from sin, for salvation.

THE DREAM – AUTHOR NOTES

MATTHEW 7:13-14

¹³ "Enter by the narrow gate; for wide is the gate and broad is the way that leads to destruction, and there are many who go in by it.

¹⁴ "Because narrow is the gate and difficult is the way which leads to life, and there are few who find it.

INTRODUCTION TO GODS GIFT OF SALVATION

Hebrews 11:1 -3

¹ Now Faith is the substance of things hoped for, the evidence of things not seen.
² For by it the elders obtained a good testimony.
³ By Faith we understand that the worlds were framed by the word of God, so that the things which are seen were not made of things which are visible.

HEAVEN OPERATES BY FAITH

Hebrews 11:1 tells us that Faith is "being sure of what we hope for and certain of what we do not see." Perhaps no other component of the Christian life is more important than Faith. We cannot purchase it, sell it or give it to our friends.

So what is Faith and what role does Faith play in the Christian life?

The dictionary defines *Faith* as "belief in, devotion to, or trust in somebody or something, especially without logical proof." It also defines *Faith* as "belief in and devotion to God."

The Bible has much more to say about Faith and how important it is. In fact, it is so important that, without Faith, we have no place with God, and it is impossible to please Him!

Hebrews 11:6 But without Faith it is impossible to please Him, for he who comes to God must believe that He is, and that He is a rewarder of those who diligently seek Him. Faith is belief in the one, true God without actually seeing Him.

HELL OPERATES BY FEAR

Faith and fear cannot exist together. Faith is described in Hebrews 11:1 as being "certain of what we do not see." It is an absolute belief that God is constantly working behind the scenes in every area of our lives, even when there is no tangible evidence to support that fact.

On the other hand, **FEAR**, simply stated, is unbelief or weak belief. As unbelief gains the upper hand in our thoughts, fear takes hold of our emotions.

OUR DELIVERANCE FROM FEAR AND WORRY IS BASED ON FAITH, WHICH IS THE VERY OPPOSITE OF UNBELIEF.

FEAR IS THE RECIPROCAL FAITH!

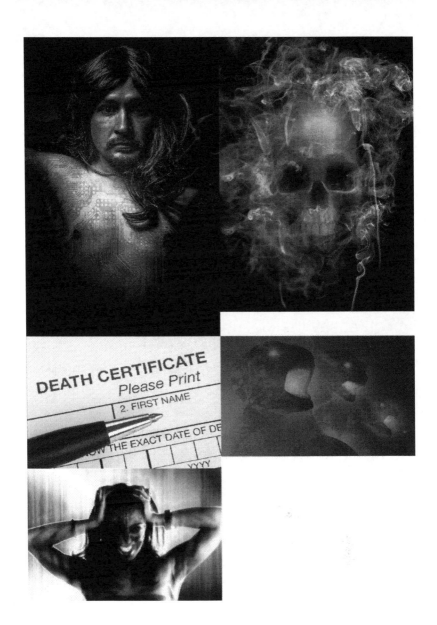

**"AS YOU READ THIS DISCOURSE YOU WILL BEGIN TO UNDERSTAND WHAT IT WILL BE LIKE IF YOU REJECT THE FREE GIFT OF SALVATION FROM GOD OUR FATHER".
(1 JOHN 4:18)**

1 JOHN 4 - TEST THE SPIRITS

Beloved, do not believe every spirit, but test the spirits, whether they are of God; because many false prophets have gone out into the world.

By this you know the Spirit of God: Every spirit that confesses that Jesus Christ has come in the flesh is of God, and every spirit that does not confess that Jesus Christ has come in the flesh is not of God.

And this is the spirit of the Antichrist, which you have heard was coming, and is now already in the world.

You are of God, little children, and have overcome them, because He who is in you is greater than he who is in the world. They are of the world.

Therefore they speak as of the world, and the world hears them.

We are of God. He who knows God hears us; he who is not of God does not hear us. By this we know the spirit of truth and the spirit of error.

GOD IS LOVE

Beloved, let us love one another, for love is of God; and everyone who loves is born of God and knows God. He who does not love does not know God, for God is love.

In this the love of God was manifested toward us, that God has sent His only begotten Son into the world, that we might live through Him.

In this is love, not that we loved God, but that He loved us and sent His Son to be the propitiation for our sins. Beloved, if God so loved us, we also ought to love one another.

No one has seen God at any time. If we love one another, God abides in us, and His love has been perfected in us.

By this we know that we abide in Him, and He in us, because He has given us of His Spirit. And we have seen and testify that the Father has sent the Son as Savior of the world.

WHOEVER CONFESSES THAT JESUS IS THE SON OF GOD, GOD ABIDES IN HIM, AND HE IN GOD.

And we have known and believed the love that God has for us. God is love, and he who abides in love abides in God, and God in him.

Love has been perfected among us in this: that we may have boldness in the Day of Judgment; because as He is, so are we in this world.

There is no fear in love; but perfect love casts out fear, because fear involves torment.

But he who fears has not been made perfect in love. We love Him because He first loved us.

If someone says, "I love God," and hates his brother, he is a liar; for he who does not love his brother whom he has seen, how can he love God whom he has not seen?

And this commandment we have from Him: that he who loves God must love his brother also.

LIFE and DEATH, THEREFORE YOU CHOSE LIFE

(Ephesians 2:5-10; Deuteronomy 30:11-20)

BY GRACE THROUGH FAITH

EPHESIANSS 2

¹ And you He made alive, who were dead in
trespasses and sins,
² in which you once walked according to
the course of this world, according to the prince of
the power of the air, the spirit who now works
in the sons of disobedience,
³ among whom also we all once conducted
ourselves in the lusts of our flesh, fulfilling the
desires of the flesh and of the mind, and were by
nature children of wrath, just as the others.
⁴ But God, who is rich in mercy, because of
His great love with which He loved us,
⁵ even when we were dead in trespasses, made
us alive together with Christ (by grace you have
been saved),
⁶ and raised us up together, and made us sit
together in the Heavenly places in Christ Jesus,
⁷ that in the ages to come He might show the
exceeding riches of His grace in His kindness
toward us in Christ Jesus.
⁸ For by grace you have been saved through
Faith, and that not of yourselves; it is the gift of
God,
⁹ not of works, lest anyone should boast.

¹⁰ For we are His workmanship, created in Christ Jesus for good works, which God prepared beforehand that we should walk in them.

THE CHOICE OF LIFE AND DEATH

DEUTERONOMY 30:11-20

¹¹ "For this commandment which I command you today is not too difficult for you, nor is it out of reach.

¹² "It is not in Heaven, that you should say, 'Who will go up to Heaven for us to get it for us and make us hear it, that we may observe it?'

¹³ "Nor is it beyond the sea, that you should say, 'Who will cross the sea for us to get it for us and make us hear it, that we may observe it?'

¹⁴ "But the word is very near you, in your mouth and in your heart, that you may observe it.

¹⁵ "See, I have set before you today life and prosperity, and death and adversity;

¹⁶ in that I command you today to love the LORD your God, to walk in His ways and to keep His commandments and His statutes and His judgments, that you may live and multiply, and that the LORD your God may bless you in the land where you are entering to possess it.

¹⁷ "But if your heart turns away and you will not obey, but are drawn away and worship other gods and serve them,

¹⁸ I declare to you today that you shall surely perish. You will not prolong your days in the land

where you are crossing the Jordan to enter and possess it.

¹⁹ "I call Heaven and earth to witness against you today, that I have set before you life and death, the blessing and the curse. So choose life in order that you may live, you and your descendants,

²⁰ by loving the LORD your God, by obeying His voice, and by holding fast to Him; for this is your life and the length of your days, that you may live in the land which the LORD swore to your fathers, to Abraham, Isaac, and Jacob, to give them."

MY NOTES & THOUGHTS

MY NOTES & THOUGHTS

ABOUT THE AUTHOR

LARRY E. HUNTER
"UNCLE BUCK THE BUMBLE BEE"
BROADCASTER & AUTHOR

In the marketing communications field for over 30 years, Larry specializes in executive coaching, professional speaking, radio & television broadcasting and most importantly, real-life, in-the-trenches mass-media marketing experience.

He has established a solid reputation as a top notch publicist, event producer and entertainment communications professional with expertise in the publishing markets. By harnessing his powerful social and media networks he nurtures a strong relationships with editors at leading publishing, advertising, press & wire services, as well as on-line outlets; and producers at major TV and radio outlets.

Larry has a knack for bringing out the best in people and is known for his savvy style and exhilarating personality where he uses his talents to launch your publicity campaigns to get you noticed. His uncanny abilities, excellent timing and publicity connections will get the word out for your events.

He draws loads of media coverage through major media outlets across the country before and during your publicity bookings. He works one-on-one to prepare you for other media events such as your local, regional and national appearances.

"There is that occasional moment, when a person is in the right place at the right time. Check me out at the ASK THE FAT MAN SHOW!

KHLP ROCKS
http://khlp.rocks/

7 Days In Hell: I Was There!
An Eyewitness Account of the True Existence Hell

First Printing, 2014

Printed in the United States of America

PUBLISHED BY
ECONO PUBLISHING, LLC
6599 Kuna Road, Kuna, Idaho 83634
E-mail: econopublishing@gmail.com
Website: www.econopublishing.com

Made in the USA
San Bernardino, CA
21 December 2015